THE STORY OF THE COLLEGE FOOTBALL
NATIONAL CHAMPIONSHIP GAME

by Barry Wilner

SportsZone
An Imprint of Abdo Publishing | abdopublishing.com

abdopublishing.com

Published by Abdo Publishing, a division of ABDO, PO Box 398166, Minneapolis, Minnesota 55439. Copyright © 2016 by Abdo Consulting Group, Inc. International copyrights reserved in all countries. No part of this book may be reproduced in any form without written permission from the publisher. SportsZone™ is a trademark and logo of Abdo Publishing.

Printed in the United States of America, North Mankato, Minnesota
052015
092015

Cover Photo: Doug James/Icon Sportswire
Interior Photos: Doug James/Icon Sportswire, 1; Ted S. Warren/AP Images, 4; AP Images, 6; Chris Carlson/AP Images, 8, 26, 40; Paul Sakuma/AP Images, 10; Kevork Djansezian/AP Images, 13; Deborah Cannon/Austin American-Statesman/AP Images, 14; John Raoux/AP Images, 16; J. Pat Carter/AP Images, 18; Mark Humphrey/AP Images, 20; Matt York/AP Images, 22; Tom Hauck/AP Images, 25; Dave Martin/AP Images, 28; David J. Phillip/AP Images, 30, 33, 38; Wilfredo Lee/AP Images, 34; Gregory Bull/AP Images, 36; Raul Demolina/AP Images, 42; Kevin Reece/AP Images, 43

Editor: Patrick Donnelly
Series Designer: Nikki Farinella

Library of Congress Control Number: 2015931483

Cataloging-in-Publication Data
Wilner, Barry.
 The story of the college football national championship game / Barry Wilner.
   p. cm. -- (Bowl games of college football)
Includes bibliographical references and index.
ISBN 978-1-62403-886-0
1. Bowl Championship Series--Juvenile literature. 2. Football--United States--Juvenile literature. 3. College sports--Juvenile literature. I. Title.
796.332--dc23
                                              2015931483

TABLE OF CONTENTS

In 1997 college football adopted the Bowl Championship Series, which finally allowed the sport to determine its national championship on the field.

BCS HISTORY:

SETTLE IT ON THE FIELD

Until 2014, Division I college football was the only major team sport in the United States that did not use a playoff to determine its champion.

For decades, the national champion was decided by a vote, either by reporters and broadcasters or by coaches. In many seasons, that led to much debate on who should be ranked number one. The media poll and the coaches' polls came up with different champions 10 times, including back-to-back years in 1990 and 1991. Fans wanted a change.

But college football officials were not eager to start a playoff system. Many argued that the players would miss too much time in the classroom. Others said that

Who's number one? That was often a much-debated topic before the BCS era.

adding extra games to the postseason would be too much of a physical burden on the players.

But eventually the push to determine a champion on the field was too strong to ignore. So the Bowl Coalition was developed in 1992, followed by the Bowl Alliance in 1995. Not every conference agreed to participate, but these moves brought college football closer to crowning a true champion. Finally, the Bowl Championship Series (BCS) was created in 1997. College football finally had a system in place that guaranteed that the top two teams would face each other for the national title.

The BCS originally used existing bowl games to decide the national champion. The title game moved each year among the Fiesta, Sugar, Orange, and Rose Bowls. In 1999, the first BCS championship game took place in the Fiesta Bowl. Tennessee beat Florida State 23–16.

In 2007, college football added a separate national championship game. That was also played in early January at one of those bowl sites. But it took place approximately one week after the actual bowl game.

NUMBER 1 VS. NUMBER 2

Before the BCS was in place, the top two teams in the final regular-season polls rarely met in a bowl game. The first time was in 1963. Number one University of Southern California (USC) knocked off second-ranked Wisconsin in the Rose Bowl on New Year's Day. In the next 24 years, only seven seasons ended with the top two teams facing off in a bowl game.

Finally, for the 2014 season, college football adopted a four-team playoff system. Six bowls were part of the new College Football Playoff. Every year, two of the bowls would serve as national semifinal games. Then the winners would meet at a predetermined site to play the championship game. Cities bid for the right to host the title game, much as they do for the Super Bowl or the basketball Final Four.

It was a long road, but major college football finally seemed to have the right system in place.

Texas quarterback Vince Young breaks away from two USC defenders in the 2006 BCS title game.

2006
INVINCIBLE VINCE
Texas vs. USC

Texas quarterback Vince Young wanted to win the Heisman Trophy. The most famous award in college sports goes to the best player in major college football. And in the 2005 season, Young thought he had a shot at winning it.

Instead, Young was beaten out by Reggie Bush, a running back at USC. So Young turned his attention to something even more important: helping his team win the national championship.

The 2006 BCS title game was set to be played at the Rose Bowl in Pasadena, California. And the matchup turned out to be a great one. Young and his fellow Longhorns faced Bush and the USC Trojans.

USC running back LenDale White struts into the end zone for one of his three touchdowns against Texas in the 2006 BCS title game.

Both teams were unbeaten. Texas won the Big 12 Conference with a 12–0 record. Meanwhile, USC took the Pac-10 crown with the same record. The teams were ranked number one and two since the beginning of the season. College football fans had been hoping for this matchup all year.

Young wanted the victory not only for himself and his teammates. He also wanted to win for longtime coach Mack Brown, who had never won a national championship.

Meanwhile, USC coach Pete Carroll and his Trojans were riding a 34-game winning streak. That run included a national championship the year before. Bush and quarterback Matt Leinart were the two most recent Heisman winners. It was the first time two holders of that trophy would play together in a college game.

"It's a perfect matchup for everyone concerned," Carroll said. "This is an extraordinary opportunity for us, to be able to play in the Rose Bowl in Pasadena. It's the goal of our program. We've done everything we can do to focus on that. It's all we could ever ask for."

They were two of the greatest programs in college football history. USC had won five Associated Press national titles, and Texas had won it twice. The result was one of the most memorable games in college football history.

Both teams were powerful on offense, and the Trojans showed it quickly. Along with Bush, USC had a strong runner in LenDale White. He scored the first touchdown of the game less than three minutes into the first quarter.

That was the only scoring of the first period. But then the Texas offense got in gear. With two touchdown runs and a field goal, the Longhorns went ahead 16–7. Mario Danelo's 43-yard field goal for USC ended the first half at 16–10. And when the Trojans scored on another touchdown run from White early in the third quarter, they went ahead by a point.

Young, who was equally dangerous on the ground as he was through the air, put Texas back on top by scooting 14 yards into the end zone. But White countered with his third touchdown of the game, a 12-yard run on a fourth-down play. Heading into the fourth quarter, USC led 24–23, the difference being a missed extra point by Texas. The national title would be decided in a wild final 15 minutes.

Carroll knew many players on the field could decide the winner. He had a few of them on his side. But Texas had Young.

"There's nobody like this," Carroll said. "There's guys that can run, there's guys that throw, there's quick guys and all that, but nobody's ever been this fast."

First, the Trojans made things even tougher for Young and the Longhorns. Bush, who fumbled in the first half to help the Longhorns stay close, scored on a darting 26-yard run to up the lead to 31–23. After Texas made a field goal, Leinart passed to receiver Dwayne Jarrett for a 22-yard score. With only 6:42 remaining in the game, USC led 38–26.

The Trojans could taste another national title. But Young was just as hungry. He led Texas on a quick drive

USC wide receiver Dwayne Jarrett, *left*, hauls in a 22-yard touchdown pass from quarterback Matt Leinart in the 2006 BCS title game.

that he capped with a 17-yard touchdown run. That made it 38–33.

The next series would define the game. USC got the ball to its 47-yard line with 2:09 left. All it needed to do was run out the clock. Texas would need to make a defensive stand to stay alive. If the Longhorns' defense could come through, the offense would get one more shot.

After three plays, USC remained two yards short. The Trojans had a big decision. They could go for those two yards and try to clinch the victory. Or they could

Vince Young celebrates Texas's victory in the 2006 BCS title game at the Rose Bowl in Pasadena, California.

punt. But Carroll did not want to put the ball in Young's hands against the exhausted Trojans defense.

The USC coach made the call to go for it. He figured that White, who was having a brilliant game, could power his way for the first down. Instead, the Texas defensive line held firm. It stopped White short.

"If you make that first down, you're squatting on the football to win the game," Carroll said. "We just missed it. By what—two inches?"

Texas quickly drove to the USC 8-yard line before stalling. It was fourth down. The national championship came down to one play.

The Trojans rushed hard to stop Young from passing, but he found an open lane and sped toward the right corner of the end zone. None of the USC players could catch him. Young raced in for the go-ahead touchdown with 19 seconds to go. Young even ran in the two-point conversion, making it 41–38.

Young, Brown, and the Longhorns had their first national championship since 1970. Young had run for 200 yards and passed for 267 more. As the game ended and Texas fans sang "The Eyes of Texas," Young hugged everyone in sight. Then he was handed the crystal Most Valuable Player (MVP) trophy.

It was not the Heisman Trophy. But Young did not mind a bit.

BAD NEWS FOR BUSH

Reggie Bush was drafted second overall by the New Orleans Saints of the National Football League (NFL) that April. Vince Young went to the Tennessee Titans one spot later. Matt Leinart was taken tenth overall by the Arizona Cardinals.

And that Heisman Trophy that Bush had won ahead of Young? It was stripped from the USC running back because he accepted money from an agent while in college. That is the only Heisman now considered vacant.

Florida running back Percy Harvin cuts through the Oklahoma defense during the 2009 BCS title game.

2009
TEBOWMANIA
Florida vs. Oklahoma

Tim Tebow was the most popular player in college football. Fans got wrapped up in "Tebowmania." The Florida Gators' quarterback and 2007 Heisman Trophy winner was a star both on the field and off. Tebow grew up with a strong religious background. He made charity work an important focus of his life outside of football.

Tebow also had already won a national title with Florida as a backup in the 2006 season. But the Gators were now his team, and they would face Big 12 champion Oklahoma in the BCS championship game. Florida went 12–1 in the regular season, winning the Southeastern Conference (SEC), the toughest conference in the United States. Tebow made big plays

Florida linebacker Brandon Hicks, *left*, hauls down Oklahoma quarterback Sam Bradford during the 2009 BCS title game.

all year with his arm and his legs. Whenever things seemed darkest for the Gators, Tebow stepped up. And Tebowmania spread throughout the country.

Well, maybe not the *entire* country. Oklahoma cornerback Dominique Franks did not think much of the Gator sensation. Franks said Tebow would only be the fourth-best quarterback in the Big 12.

"I think our quarterbacks are better," Franks said. "Just the way they conduct themselves and how they play on the field. I just think, playing against those guys, it's a lot harder to prepare for those guys than it is for Tebow."

Tebow laughed off Franks's comments. But he carried an extra sense of purpose onto the field at Sun Life Stadium in Miami. The Sooners' offense had averaged 54 points during the season, a college football record. But the Florida defense played well. Neither team scored in the first quarter. Finally Tebow got Florida on the board with a 20-yard pass to Louis Murphy in the second quarter.

But Oklahoma struck right back. Quarterback Sam Bradford, who had beaten out Tebow for the Heisman that year, hit tight end Jermaine Gresham for a 6-yard touchdown. The game was tied 7–7 at halftime.

The second half was often when Tebow, star running back Percy Harvin, and the Gators' defense usually did their best work. This game would be no different.

"I wanted to do whatever I could to help my team win this game," Tebow said, "and if I was trying to run and run some people over, to get the crowd into it, to get the momentum, then that was what I was going to try to do."

Tim Tebow throws a pass over Oklahoma defensive end Auston English during the 2009 BCS title game.

Harvin's 2-yard run was the only scoring in the third quarter. The fast, hard-hitting Florida defense continued to slow Oklahoma's usually unstoppable attack. But the Gators could hold the Sooners down for only so long. Bradford and Gresham connected for another touchdown. With just over 12 minutes remaining, the game was tied 14–14.

On the next series, Harvin—who rushed for 122 yards on a sore ankle that night—ripped off a 52-yard run. That led to Jonathan Phillips's 27-yard field goal and a 17–14 Gators lead.

Could Florida hold on against the mighty Sooners' no-huddle offense? Yes, indeed. The Gators harassed Bradford with a strong pass rush. And when Tebow got the ball back, he guided the Gators on a clinching drive.

Florida finished off the drive with a play that was classic Tebow. He took two steps toward the line as if to run, which was not unusual—Tebow rushed for 109 yards in the game. But then he pulled up short, jumped, and passed over the onrushing defenders to receiver David Nelson. The 4-yard touchdown pass gave Florida a 24–14 lead with 3:07 left.

Oklahoma was done. And just to make sure, when Florida ran out the clock, Tebow carried the ball on the final six plays. The Gators were national champions once again, this time riding Tebowmania to the title.

TEBOW'S TALK TURNS THE TIDE

With the score tied at halftime, Tim Tebow made a loud and excited speech to his teammates. He shouted, "We've got 30 minutes for the rest of our lives. We get the ball, I promise you one thing, we're going to hit somebody and we're going to take it downfield for a touchdown, I guarantee you that. Let's go!"

Auburn quarterback Cam Newton fires a pass against Oregon in the 2011 BCS title game.

2011
CAM'S CROWN
Auburn vs. Oregon

Most football fans had never heard of Cam Newton. Those who did likely forgot about him. He was on the Florida Gators during their 2008 championship season. But Newton did not play much. Then he was charged with stealing another student's computer. The charges were dropped, but Newton still left Florida. He spent the 2009 season at tiny Blinn College in Texas. It was a long way from the SEC.

But coaches at Auburn did not forget about Newton. They watched as he led his team to the junior college national title. They figured he could help their team, so they gave him a scholarship for the 2010 season.

However, even they could not have predicted how much Newton would help the Tigers.

The strong-armed, strong-legged, strong-willed quarterback ran away with the Heisman Trophy. And by season's end, he had brought the Tigers to within one game of their first national title since 1957. They just had to beat Oregon first.

"I look back at it and consider it a blessing," Newton said of his long and winding journey. "I think that whole process has made me stronger, and I opened my eyes to the fact of who is in this process for me and whether it is family members, friends, or whatever. I learned about so many people that are very close to me."

Auburn had won the mighty SEC with a 13–0 record. Included were victories against strong teams such as South Carolina, Louisiana State University (LSU), and Arkansas. Then the Tigers made a stunning comeback from a 24-point hole on the road to beat archrival Alabama 28–27. They wiped out South Carolina 56–17 in the SEC championship game, setting up a date with Oregon in Phoenix for the national title.

The Ducks had run around, over, and through every opponent in going 12–0. They scored at least 37 points in all but one game with a fast-paced offense led by All-America running back LaMichael James. Oregon

Oregon quarterback Darron Thomas scans the field in search of an open receiver against Auburn in the 2011 BCS title game.

coach Chip Kelly knew his team could score against anyone. But he also knew that his Ducks would have to slow down Newton to win their first national title.

"I remember watching him in pregame warm-ups and seeing him throw," Kelly said. "I said, 'Holy smokes, this guy is going to make an [NFL] quarterback.' He can make all the throws. And then, unfortunately when you have to go against him, if you defend all their throws he has the ability to pull it down and run. . . . He's the complete package at the quarterback spot."

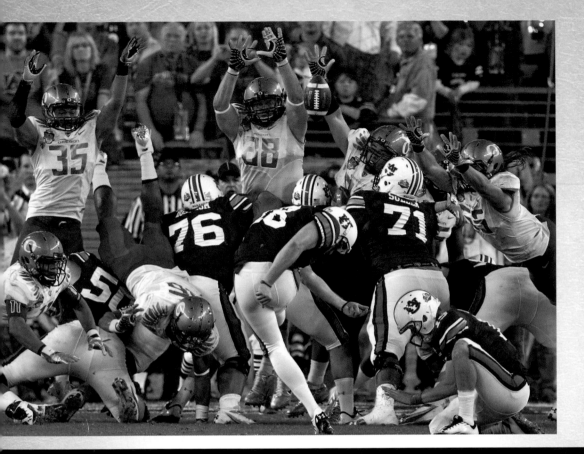

Auburn's Wes Byrum, *center*, kicks the game-winning field goal against Oregon in the 2011 BCS title game.

The stage was set for Auburn's quarterback or Oregon's running back to take the spotlight. Instead, something odd happened. Oregon quarterback Darron Thomas and Auburn running back Michael Dyer stepped up and did much of the offensive work.

Even more unusual, this championship game featuring two high-flying offenses was mostly decided by defense. The first quarter was scoreless. That made the fans at the University of Phoenix Stadium restless. Where were all the points?

Both offenses got going in the second quarter, at least for a while. Oregon got on the scoreboard first with a 26-yard field goal by Rob Beard. Then Newton found Kodi Burns for a 35-yard touchdown pass and a 7–3 lead.

Back came the Ducks. Thomas and Jeff Maehl combined for an exciting 81-yard pass play. Oregon then scored on an 8-yard pass from Thomas to James. The Ducks even made a two-point conversion. Beard, the kicker, ran into the end zone on a trick play for an 11–7 lead.

But Newton brought the Tigers right down the field. They looked ready to retake the load. On fourth down from the 1, though, Newton's pass to Eric Smith was too low. Oregon took over.

But not for long. Auburn defensive lineman Mike Blanc tackled James in the end zone for a safety to make it 11–9. Oregon then had to kick to Auburn. On the next drive, Newton hit Emory Blake from 30 yards out, and Auburn led 16–11.

But after that wide-open second quarter, defense and the kicking game would rule the day. Wes Byrum's third-quarter field goal gave Auburn an eight-point edge.

Cam Newton, *left,* has a big laugh as Auburn coach Gene Chizik gets a Gatorade bath after the Tigers won the 2011 BCS title game against Oregon.

The Tigers defense held, but the Ducks had another trick play up their sleeves. This time, punter Jackson Rice threw an 11-yard pass to Marvin Johnson for a first down.

But then something happened to the Ducks that they never could have imagined. They could not finish the job. Oregon got to the Auburn 1 but was stopped on fourth down.

Deep into the fourth quarter, Auburn clung to its 19–11 lead. Oregon got another chance to tie it after Newton lost a fumble. Thomas completed a 29-yard pass on fourth down. Then he hit James for a 2-yard score with 2:33 remaining. Needing another two-point conversion, the Ducks got that, too, on a pass to Maehl.

Tied at 19–19, the game appeared to be headed for overtime. But Dyer, the Tigers' freshman running back, had other plans. He took a handoff and seemed to be tackled, but he was lying on top of another player, not on the ground. So Dyer got up and sprinted 37 yards to the Oregon 23.

Auburn got to the 1-yard line, ran down the clock, and called out Byrum. The Tigers kicker booted a 19-yard field goal as time expired to give Auburn the national championship.

"Anything is possible," Newton said. "I guarantee you five or six months ago, nobody would have bet their last dollar to say that Auburn University is winning the national championship. And now, on January 10, 2011, we're smiling."

NO DOUBTING THOMAS

Cam Newton won the Heisman Trophy in 2010. But another quarterback nearly stole the show in the BCS title game. Oregon's Darron Thomas had only topped 300 yards passing once that year. But against Auburn with the title on the line, Thomas completed 27 of 40 passes for a career-high 363 yards. He also threw for two touchdowns and a two-point conversion.

Alabama quarterback A. J. McCarron sets up to throw a pass against Notre Dame during the 2013 BCS title game.

2013
ROLL TIDE 3
Alabama vs. Notre Dame

I t was a classic matchup of great college football programs. Alabama and Notre Dame each had won eight national championships. In the 2012 season they were ranked first and second most of the year. The 12–0 Fighting Irish came into the game ranked number one. They were one spot ahead of the 12–1 Crimson Tide.

Anyone with an interest in the sport was eager to see the game at SunLife Stadium in Miami. Both teams had taken the hard road to get there. Notre Dame had beaten such powerful teams as Oklahoma, USC, Michigan, and Michigan State. Alabama had won the SEC, knocking off third-ranked Georgia in the conference title game.

Coach Nick Saban's Crimson Tide were the defending national champions and were looking for their third title in four years. The SEC had won six straight national crowns. Alabama led the country in total defense and rushing defense. It was second against the pass. Only Notre Dame had given up fewer points per game.

But the expected defensive battle did not happen. Blame the Crimson Tide's offense. From the very beginning of one of the most-watched championship games in the sport's history, it was a blowout.

Running back Eddie Lacy scored on a 20-yard dash to get Alabama started. His touchdown finished off an 82-yard opening drive. It was the longest drive Notre Dame allowed all season.

Then Alabama quarterback A. J. McCarron threw a 3-yard touchdown pass to Michael Williams. Less than nine minutes into the BCS championship game, Notre Dame was in trouble.

The Irish could not recover. Alabama just poured it on, getting a 1-yard touchdown run by T. J. Yeldon and another scoring pass from McCarron, this time to Lacy. By halftime, it was 28–0 and Notre Dame was done.

Alabama made it 35–0 on another McCarron touchdown pass—one of four on the night for the junior quarterback. The Irish finally found the end zone, but

Alabama running back Eddie Lacy celebrates after scoring a touchdown against Notre Dame in the 2013 BCS title game.

Alabama players celebrate after the Crimson Tide blew out Notre Dame 42–14 in the 2013 BCS title game.

the Alabama defense did not allow Notre Dame any running room. The Irish gained just 32 yards on the ground, 170 below their season average.

Meanwhile, Alabama gained 529 yards, including 265 on the ground, against a tough Irish defense that no opponent had solved the entire season. The Tide held the ball for more than 38 minutes. And, of course, Alabama scored 42 points against a team that had allowed only 124 during 12 regular-season games.

When it was over and the confetti streamed down on the field, all the Notre Dame players, fans, and coaches could do was shake their heads at how good Alabama was. The Tide had won back-to-back championships for the third time in school history. Saban, who led LSU to the 2003 championship, became the first coach to win BCS title games at two schools. His players often made fun of Saban because he rarely smiled. But after beating Notre Dame, even he wore a grin. His Crimson Tide was back on top.

CHAMPIONSHIP DROUGHT

Alabama added to its national championship total, but Notre Dame has been stuck on eight since 1988, when it beat West Virginia in the Fiesta Bowl to clinch the title. The Irish never had gone more than 18 years without winning the college football championship since national polling began. But as of 2015, their latest streak was 27 years and counting.

Auburn quarterback Nick Marshall, 14, releases the ball as he is hit by Florida State's Terrance Smith, 24, and Mario Edwards during the 2014 BCS title game.

2014
SEMINOLES SQUEAKER
Florida State vs. Auburn

The new College Football Playoff system was set to begin in the 2014 season. What better place to play the final BCS National Championship Game than Pasadena? That is where bowl games began in 1902. And what better matchup than Auburn against Florida State? Auburn had gone 12-1 and won the SEC. That conference had produced the previous seven national champions. Meanwhile, top-ranked Florida State was the nation's only unbeaten team.

The excitement built because both teams could score lots of points. The Seminoles were led by Heisman Trophy winner Jameis Winston at quarterback. The Tigers featured star running back Tre Mason. He rushed for 1,621 yards and 22 touchdowns for the top-ranked

Florida State quarterback Jameis Winston throws a pass against Auburn in the 2014 BCS title game.

ground game in the country. But Florida State had allowed only 10.7 points per game that season. It gave up seven points or fewer seven times. Although Auburn had scored at least 30 points 11 times that year, the Tigers knew it would be tougher to find the end zone against Florida State.

Even though kickoff came approximately one month after both teams had last played, the Seminoles and Tigers were sharp. Auburn was a lot sharper early on, taking a 21-3 lead as Nick Marshall threw two touchdown passes. The Tigers were not backing down against the number one team in the land.

Florida State made it 21-10 before halftime. Then the Seminoles climbed to within one point when Winston threw a touchdown pass early in the fourth quarter.

The Rose Bowl was rocking. Auburn fans relaxed a bit when Cody Parkey made a short field goal with 4:42 remaining for a 24-20 lead. Then came one of the wildest finishes in the sport's history.

Kermit Whitfield received the ensuing kickoff. Eleven seconds later, he was in the other end zone. Whitfield ran up the left side, got a big block from Karlos Williams, and never was touched on a 100-yard return. His teammates mobbed him in the end zone, but this incredible game was not close to being over.

Trailing 27-24, back came Auburn. Florida State's defense was tiring, and Mason broke through it on a 37-yard run to regain the lead 31-27.

"It felt storybook again," said Auburn defensive tackle Gabe Wright, whose team had been behind a lot

Florida State wide receiver Kelvin Benjamin, *top*, stretches to catch the game-winning touchdown pass against Auburn in the 2014 BCS title game.

during the season but had always rallied. "It really felt like we were going to bring it out again."

With one defensive stand, the Tigers might have held on. But this was Florida State, whose freshman quarterback never gave up. Winston had not played well for much of the night, but he hit six of seven passes on an 80-yard drive. His 49-yard completion to Rashad Greene was the big play. Only 1:19 remained when the Seminoles had started the drive. Now, just a few seconds were on the clock as Winston stood at the 2-yard line with the national championship hanging in the balance.

He dropped back to pass, then fired high over the middle. Wide receiver Kelvin Benjamin stretched his 6-foot-5-inch frame. He came down with the ball in the end zone with 13 seconds to go. Florida State was on top of the college football world with a 34–31 victory.

"Once the ball is in the air on that post route, I've got to go get it, and I did," Benjamin said. "Simple as that."

Winston and his buddies could celebrate the school's first BCS title since 1999 and its third ever. And the college football world looked forward to more excitement with the new playoff format.

CLOSE CALL

To reach the BCS championship game, Auburn first needed to beat Alabama in their yearly matchup, known as the Iron Bowl. With the game tied 28–28, Alabama attempted a 57-yard field goal on the game's final play. But the kick came up short, and Auburn's Chris Davis returned it 100 yards down the left sideline for a touchdown and a shocking 34–28 victory.

TIMELINE

1936

The Associated Press begins polling sportswriters to determine college football's national champion.

1950

United Press begins polling college football coaches to decide a national champion.

1954

The first split national champions vote occurs, with the media selecting Ohio State and the coaches voting for the University of California, Los Angeles (UCLA).

1963

Top-ranked University of Southern California (USC) defeats number two Wisconsin in the Rose Bowl on New Year's Day. It is the first-ever bowl game featuring the top two teams in the country.

1988

Number two Miami defeats top-ranked Oklahoma in the Orange Bowl to win the national championship. It is only the eighth time in 25 years that the top two teams in the nation faced off in a bowl game.

1991

For the second consecutive year, the national championship voting is split. The media selects Miami, whereas the coaches vote for Washington.

1992

The Bowl Coalition is created to find a better way to determine a national champion. Two major conferences—the Big Ten and Pac-10—decide not to join.

1995

The Bowl Alliance replaces the Bowl Coalition, but the Big Ten and Pac-10 remain holdouts.

1997

The BCS standings are created. The standings use computer rankings, the media and coaches' polls, team records, and strength of schedule to determine the order of the standings.

1999

The first BCS title game using the bowls is played, with Tennessee beating Florida State 23–16 in the Fiesta Bowl on January 4.

2004

Louisiana State University (LSU) wins the BCS title game against Oklahoma, but the media poll ranks USC number one.

2004

A national championship game separate from the bowls is approved.

2007

Florida beats Ohio State 41–14 in the first BCS championship game played after the bowl games.

2013

Alabama wins its third BCS championship game in four years in a 42–14 rout of Notre Dame.

2014

College football adopts a new playoff system that includes the top four teams in the country.

2015

The first College Football Playoff semifinals take place on New Year's Day. Fourth-ranked Ohio State upsets number one Alabama in the Sugar Bowl, and second-ranked Oregon beats number three Florida State in the Rose Bowl.

2015

Ohio State wins the first College Football Playoff with a 42–20 win against Oregon in Arlington, Texas.

BOWL RECORDS

Most total yards
467, Vince Young, Texas vs. USC, 2006

Most pass attempts
51, Chris Weinke, Florida State vs. Oklahoma, 2001

Most completions
30, Vince Young, Texas vs. USC, 2006

Most passing yards
365, Matt Leinart, USC vs. Texas, 2006

Most touchdown passes
5, Matt Leinart, USC vs. Oklahoma, 2005

Most rushing yards
246, Ezekiel Elliott, Ohio State vs. Oregon, 2015

Longest run from scrimmage
65 yards, Chris "Beanie" Wells, Ohio State vs. LSU, 2008

Most receptions
11, Kellen Winslow Jr., Miami (Florida) vs. Ohio State, 2003

Most receiving yards
199, Peerless Price, Tennessee vs. Florida State, 1999; and Andre Johnson, Miami (Florida) vs. Nebraska, 2002.

Longest reception
81 yards, Jeff Maehl, Oregon vs. Auburn, 2011

Most tackles
18, James Laurinaitis, Ohio State vs. LSU, 2008

Most sacks
3, Derrick Harvey, Florida vs. Ohio State, 2007

Most interceptions
2, Sean Taylor, Miami vs. Ohio State, 2003; and Javier Arenas, Alabama vs. Texas, 2010

Most points scored
55; USC 55, Oklahoma 19, 2005

Fewest points allowed
0; Alabama 21, LSU 0, 2012

*through the 2015 National Championship Game

QUOTES AND ANECDOTES

In 2012, two teams from the same conference played for the BCS championship: Alabama and LSU of the Southeastern Conference (SEC). That did not sit well with the conferences whose teams were shut out of the game.

Oklahoma State coach Mike Gundy could not figure out why a rematch of two SEC teams would be more fun than his high-scoring Cowboys facing the strong defense of either Alabama or LSU.

"For whatever reason, people decided they wanted to see a rematch of LSU and Alabama," Gundy said. "There obviously weren't enough people who wanted to see the Big 12 champion against the SEC champion."

Florida State offensive lineman Michael Scheerhorn raised $12,000 to help 12-year-old Jayden Laspada, a Seminoles fan who had cancer, attend the 2014 game. Scheerhorn's brother, Daniel, also had cancer when he was a child.

Only one team played in three straight BCS championship games, and that happened at the very beginning. Florida State lost to Tennessee in 1999, beat Virginia Tech in 2000, and lost to Oklahoma in 2001.

"All I knew was the whistle wasn't blowing and my coach was saying 'Go!'"—Auburn running back Michael Dyer on his long run to set up the winning field goal in the 2011 title game

GLOSSARY

alliance

A group working together toward a common goal.

confetti

Small pieces of colorful paper thrown into the air in celebration.

freshman

A first-year player.

invincible

Impossible to beat.

junior college

A two-year school where teams also play sports.

pylon

A marker placed where the goal line meets the out-of-bounds line.

rivals

Teams that play each other often and have an ongoing competition.

tradition

The way things have been done for years.

two-point conversion

A play instead of a kick after a touchdown; a kick is worth only one point.

vacant

Not awarded, as in the 2005 Heisman Trophy.

FOR MORE INFORMATION

Further Reading

Holmes, Parker. *The Alabama Crimson Tide*. New York: PowerKids Press, 2013.

Howell, Brian. *Auburn Tigers*. Minneapolis, MN: Abdo Publishing, 2013.

Roselius, J. Chris. *Texas Longhorns*. Minneapolis, MN: Abdo Publishing, 2013.

Websites

To learn more about Bowl Games of College Football, visit **booklinks.abdopublishing.com**. These links are routinely monitored and updated to provide the most current information available.

Place to Visit

College Football Hall of Fame
250 Marietta Street NW
Atlanta, Georgia 30313
404-880-4800
www.cfbhall.com
This hall of fame and museum highlights the greatest players and moments in the history of college football. Relocated from South Bend, Indiana, in 2014, it includes multiple galleries, a theater, and an interactive area where fans can test their football skills.

INDEX

About the Author

Barry Wilner has written 49 books, including many for young readers. He is a sports writer for the Associated Press and has covered major events such as the Super Bowl, Olympics, and World Cup. He lives in Garnerville, New York.